I think Dave Ramos's differentiation theory in Decide One Thing *is very interesting.*

What's the one thing your organization can do, or provide, or make, better than anybody else? If you can figure that out, you're halfway to greatness—and if you can deliver on the promise, you're there.

This book is full of ideas that will kindle the imagination of any leader.

—KEN BLANCHARD

coauthor of *The One Minute Manager®* and *Trust Works!*

DECIDE

ONE

THING

THE ONE THING *EVERY* EXECUTIVE TEAM
MUST DECIDE

DAVE RAMOS

Advantage®

Published by Advantage, Charleston, South Carolina.
Member of Advantage Media Group.

ADVANTAGE is a registered trademark and the Advantage colophon is a trademark of Advantage Media Group, Inc.

Shiftpoints® is a registered trademark and the Shiftpoints Logo is a trademark of Shiftpoints, Inc.

Printed in the United States of America.

ISBN: 978-159932-430-2
LCCN: 2013942334

This publication is designed to provide accurate and authoritative information in regard to the subject matter covered. It is sold with the understanding that the publisher is not engaged in rendering legal, accounting, or other professional services. If legal advice or other expert assistance is required, the services of a competent professional person should be sought.

Advantage Media Group is proud to be a part of the Tree Neutral® program. Tree Neutral offsets the number of trees consumed in the production and printing of this book by taking proactive steps such as planting trees in direct proportion to the number of trees used to print books. To learn more about Tree Neutral, please visit **www.treeneutral.com**. To learn more about Advantage's commitment to being a responsible steward of the environment, please visit **www.advantagefamily.com/green**

Advantage Media Group is a publisher of business, self-improvement, and professional development books and online learning. We help entrepreneurs, business leaders, and professionals share their Stories, Passion, and Knowledge to help others Learn & Grow. Do you have a manuscript or book idea that you would like us to consider for publishing? Please visit **advantagefamily.com** or call **1.866.775.1696**.

CONTENTS

B.L.U.F.

The United States military has millions of acronyms.

My favorite is B.L.U.F.—which stands for Bottom Line Up Front.

So, here is the bottom line: organizations must be good at lots of things. However, a differentiating competitive advantage comes from being great at One Thing. Not just great—*differentiatingly* great.

The rest of this book makes the case for this idea, presents a range of case studies to help you understand some of the options, and outlines the process for deciding.

The one thing **every** executive team must decide is, "What is your One Thing?"

INTRODUCTION

There are two kinds of people in the world.

Those who *always* read the introduction section of a book…like my wife, and those who *never* read the introduction…like me!

So if you are an introduction reader, this section is for you!

Several years ago, I was having breakfast with Ken Thornton, a retired IBM senior executive and a member of the SHIFTPOINTS Advisory Board, soliciting his advice about how to build the business.

"Dave—you need to develop a methodology, and you need to write a book."

Those words hit me hard. The 20-minute drive home felt like a time warp. I remember thinking, "Write a book? Where do I even begin?"

As I tried to start writing, all I could think of was the hilarious movie *Throw Momma from the Train*, starring Billy Crystal and Danny DeVito. In the movie, Billy Crystal plays an author with writer's block. Over and over, he types out the first line of his book.

"The night was …"

And over and over, he rips the paper from his typewriter in frustration. He is stuck.

Like Crystal in the movie, I had a lot of fits and starts. I have a degree in accounting, not literature.

Eventually, however, I found my voice. I adopted a writing style that I first learned from the advertising copywriters I worked with back in my Nortel Networks days.

Short, punchy sentences. Often without verbs.

It drives the grammarians and Microsoft Word crazy, but it works for me.

I hope you like it.

A lot!

EXECUTIVE TEAMS, PROPHETS, AND CHANGE AGENTS

There are millions of books on leadership, and there are millions of executive coaches.

So why is there such a leadership void?

Because leadership is a team sport.

Most leadership books are written as if there were one supreme leader and everyone else is simply a follower.

Most coaches only work with one leader, as if that will make the team better.

But leadership simply does not work that way.

That's why SHIFTPOINTS' model is to work with the entire leadership team of an organization.

However, the Decide One Thing process is really the purview and responsibility of the CEO and the senior executive team.

So this book is specifically written for the executive team...to go through as a team!

While this book is designed for the executive team, in some cases, the reader of this book will not be the CEO or a member of the executive team.

Most likely, you are a prophet and/or a change agent, and every organization needs people like you. You push the envelope. Say what needs to be said. Poke and prod. Nudge and cajole.

We have some advice for prophets and change agents:

- Buy copies of this book for your CEO and his or her direct reports.

- Start a grassroots movement with other prophets and change agents.

- Lead brainstorming sessions about what your organization's One Thing might be.

- Be an internal champion for the cause of being "differentiation-driven."

- Help your own team become differentiatingly great.

Do these things, and pretty soon you might actually become a member of the executive team.

CHAPTER ONE

SHIFT POINTS

ONLY ONE THING CAN BE THE MAIN THING.

SHIFT POINTS

It probably won't take long for you to figure out that I'm a car guy.

My mom is German. I'll never forget my first trip to Germany. I was ten years old. Within a few minutes of our arrival, we pulled out onto the Autobahn and zoooooom!

A silver Porsche 911 passed us like we were standing still. I was hooked.

So when I started my company, it was just natural for me to use car-related analogies in my work.

Our clients are mid sized, high-growth organizations, run by what we call "Fast Lane Leaders."

The majority of our work has been helping clients who were at a strategic inflection point.

We call them shift points.

For some, their growth had plateaued. Others wanted to take their organizations "to the next level."

All of them were struggling to break out of the competitive pack.

Ultimately, these organizations—specifically their senior executive teams—had some big decisions to make:

They could be disappointingly mediocre at everything, or become differentiatingly great at One Thing.

They could dabble in dozens of markets…or dominate One Market.

They could remain fragmented and inefficient…or align everyone in One Direction.

They could continue backstabbing and undermining… or come together as One Team.

They could stay with the herd on the wide road, or make their own way on the Narrow One.

Perhaps your organization is also at a shift point. Perhaps the recession has taken its toll. Perhaps your people are running on fumes. Perhaps the competition has passed you by.

If so, this book will lay out a clear choice.

DIFFERENTIATION-DRIVEN

There are many things that can (and do) drive organizations.

In our experience, the real high-performance organizations are differentiation-driven.

SHIFTPOINTS has spent the last ten years working to answer two questions:

What (exactly) is a high-performance organization?

What does it take to build one?

The process started with an intense period of reading and research. Conservatively, we have read 100 books on the subject.

To supplement our "100 Books" research program, we had conversations with over 100 CEOs. These CEO conversations were tremendously helpful as we worked to understand what it really takes to build a high-performance organization.

In addition, we developed a High-Performance Organization Survey to provide hard data to supplement the anecdotal research.

Ultimately, we concluded that high-performance organizations are "differentiation-driven."

Differentiation-driven organizations are unique and very rare.

First, they have identified something (which we call One Thing) that is their defining differentiation. Second, they use their One Thing to align everything in the organization:

- They have compelling corporate identities and often become iconic brands.

- They have tightly focused corporate strategies and create truly unique products and services.

- They recruit, retain, and unleash the talents of the very best people in their industry, who share a unique DNA.

- They manage the organization with incredible clarity, so everyone is driving in the same direction.

Finally, differentiation-driven organizations win. Far more often than their undifferentiated, unfocused, and uninspiring competitors.

Differentiation-driven organizations are unique, aligned, and intensely focused. That's why they win.

Our model is simple:
Decide One Thing. Align Everything. Win!

WARNING LIGHTS

....

SHIFTPOINTS starts engagements with a comprehensive diagnostic of the organization's current performance.

Of course, one of the primary things we look at is differentiation.

Your car's dashboard has warning lights that alert you when something is wrong. (If you are like most people, you ignore them for a long time before taking action.)

Likewise, your organization has warning lights that alert you when your differentiation is low. These are some of the most common ones:

- Low win rates

- Heavy price discounts

- Plateaued growth

- Trouble recruiting top talent

- High employee turnover

- Low employee engagement

- High delivery variability

- Low customer retention

- Low margins

- Low brand awareness

Perhaps your organization is seeing some of these warning lights. (If you are like most organizations, you have been ignoring them for a long time.)

Perhaps you have even hired consultants to help you fix one or more of these issues. My hunch is that it did not work, probably because the consultant misdiagnosed the problem.

For example, hiring an HR consultant to help you with employee engagement won't really work—because engagement isn't the problem. It is a symptom of a much larger and more complicated problem.

These warning lights are all symptoms of low differentiation. Solving them requires a comprehensive diagnostic and uniquely integrated approach.

Decide One Thing. Align Everything. Win!

TEN EASY QUESTIONS

My father-in-law taught Old Testament courses at a conservative Bible college. He was legendary for being a difficult and demanding professor. All of his students remember his pop quizzes, which always had the same feature.

Ten easy questions.

Of course, they were never easy.

To evaluate your organization's current level of differentiation, consider taking the SHIFTPOINTS Differentiation Index assessment.

The Differentiation Index is comprised of ten (not so easy) questions.

You can take the assessment for free, but you must register and request a company ID. To start the process, contact us at start@SHIFTPOINTS.com.

Once you have completed the assessment, SHIFTPOINTS will provide a report of your results, including a competitive benchmark, which compares your organization with every other organization that has completed the assessment.

Decide One Thing. Align Everything. Win!

CHAPTER TWO

WHY ONE THING?

IT IS BETTER TO BE DIFFERENTIATINGLY
GREAT AT ONE THING THAN
DISAPPOINTINGLY MEDIOCRE
AT DOZENS OF THINGS.

ONE QUESTION

Whenever I meet a new executive, I always start with the same question.

"How do you differentiate your firm?"

You'd be surprised how many people can't answer that question.

Most organizations look alike, sound alike, and act alike. Their products are the same. Their brands are bland.

They disappear into a vanilla sea of sameness.

You go to a trade show, but every booth looks the same. You go home with a bag of giveaways, but end up giving them all away.

You shop for gas, but every station seems the same. You debate crossing the street but can't justify the pain.

You go to a networking event, but everyone sounds the same. You unload your pocket of business cards but can't remember anyone's name.

You board the plane, but every airline sounds the same. Flight attendants offer you peanuts, and the kid next to you is driving you insane.

You review the proposals, but all the vendors blend together. The sales reps show up, and you just yak about the weather.

Most books about differentiation focus on being different. This one focuses on being better.

Not just a little bit better…not just great…but differentiatingly great.

Because it is good to be different, but it is great to be differentiatingly great.

Decide One Thing. Align Everything. Win!

- Does your organization blend into the bland vanilla sea of sameness?

- How would you answer the differentiation question?

- Are you experiencing any of the warning lights of low differentiation?

CORPORATE DIFFERENTIATION

The word "corporate" has taken on a negative connotation.

We're from corporate...and we're here to help.

However, the main reason that most organizations struggle with differentiation is that they have not done the corporate-level work.

Most organizations focus on differentiating their products but never tackle the task of differentiating their company.

Often, the subject of differentiation is just delegated to the marketing department to work on with the advertising agency.

"Make our brochures better."

However, your corporate differentiation is really something far bigger and more strategic than just marketing. Done properly, it impacts everything in your organization, from human resources to finance to how you keep score.

It is your *corporate* differentiation that creates one powerful and compelling brand identity. It clarifies who the organization is and what you stand for.

It is your *corporate* differentiation that aligns all of your tactics into One Strategy.

It is your *corporate* differentiation that unifies all of your people into One Team.

It is your *corporate* differentiation that integrates all of your products and services into One Portfolio.

So creating a corporate-level differentiation is vitally important. But it is also really hard.

Completing this difficult work is the responsibility of the senior executive team.

You could even say that it is Job One.

Differentiation-driven organizations are good at many things—but decide to become differentiatingly great at One Thing.

Decide One Thing. Align Everything. Win!

- Does your organization have a corporate-level differentiation?

- Is differentiation seen as a "marketing issue" or a corporate strategy goal?

- Do you have a powerful and compelling brand identity?

THE CHALLENGE

But if differentiation is so important, why are most organizations so vanilla?

Because building a differentiation-driven organization is hard.

Here are a few of the most common challenges:

- Organizations are complex entities, and it is hard to find One Thing that everyone can agree on.

- Organizations are constantly changing, merging, divesting, etc., so making a decision about a corporate-level differentiation seems like a moving target.

- Most organizations have divisions, and often the division general managers have more power than corporate headquarters. Thus, there is a tendency to fight "corporate" initiatives.

- Most organizations operate in multiple geographies, and it is hard to get all of the geography heads to agree on one corporate differentiation that works globally.

- Most branding firms don't have the strategic breadth that is required to address differentiation at the corporate level. In addition, many people equate differentiation with creating a logo.

- Creating a corporate-level differentiation is hard, so executive teams procrastinate the decision. Differentiation is always important but rarely urgent.

- Many executive teams don't work well enough together to effectively solve strategic problems. They fight and disagree, and the differentiation decision gets stuck in a strategic stalemate.

- Big strategic trends, like globalization and the Internet, have made every industry massively more competitive. Thus, finding something to differentiate your organization is a challenge...all the good ideas seem to have already been taken.

No one has ever devised a simple yet powerful methodology to help executive teams develop and then actualize a corporate-level differentiation...until now.

Decide One Thing. Align Everything. Win!

- Do you believe that your entire organization could ever agree to One Thing?

- Does it seem like all of the good differentiation ideas have already been taken by your competitors?

- Would you consider using an outside facilitator to break the strategic stalemate?

THE ONE THING

SHIFTPOINTS developed a methodology for creating a corporate-level differentiation that we call Decide One Thing.

Here is the basic premise:

Every organization is good at many things.

But differentiation comes from being great at One Thing.

This is a radically new and different approach.

Unlike traditional branding models, this model does not focus on creating a new logo, some pithy messaging, and a new brochure. We all know that approach doesn't work. We even have a phrase for it.

"Putting lipstick on a pig."

So our starting point is to identify something that you can become differentiatingly great at. Then you must use that concept to align everything in your organization to turn that concept into reality.

You won't become great just by *saying* that you are great. It requires incredible discipline and dogmatic leadership.

Any study of *individual* greatness reveals that people pay a high price for achieving greatness.

This is also true for *organizational* greatness.

It is extremely hard to become great at something, but it is impossible to become great at twenty-seven things. Therefore, you must choose something—One Thing—to become great at, and then be willing to pay the price for actually achieving greatness.

And, of course, this requires intense effort over a really long period of time. Many people—and organizations—say they want to be great, but don't have the determination required to achieve it.

There is a headline from an old Nike ad that captures this idea perfectly, *"One man's workout is another man's warm-up."*

Focus on achieving greatness. That's what truly differentiates.

Decide One Thing. Align Everything. Win!

- Is your organization truly committed to achieving greatness?

- What do you think achieving greatness will cost you?

- Is everyone—especially every executive—willing to pay the price?

YOU MUST DECIDE

The reason we say "Decide One Thing" is to reinforce the notion that you must decide.

There are many options, but you have to choose One of them.

Which, by definition, means that you are *not* choosing the other ones.

You can be the cheapest or the most expensive. But not both.

You can be the biggest or the smallest. But not both.

You can have the most or the fewest. But not both.

Walmart chose price as their One Thing. They have good service, good selection, and good design. But Walmart has differentiatingly great prices. Every day Walmart focuses on lowering costs and passing along the savings, "helping their customers save money and live better."

Nordstrom chose customer service. They have good prices and good selection. But Nordstrom has differentiatingly great service. The corporation's heroes are sales clerks who go way, way beyond the call of duty to serve their customers.

Apple chose product design as their One Thing. They have limited selection, but "insanely great" design. Their stores are cool. Their packaging is cool. Their ads are cool. Even their power supplies are cool.

Amazon chose product selection. They have good service, good prices, but unbelievable "A to Z" selection. They started by applying Web technology to books. Now they carry everything from air conditioners to Zippo lighters.

BMW chose performance. They have good quality, good design, but incredible driving performance. They are "The Ultimate Driving Machine." They have interviews with suspension engineers on their website.

Lexus chose quality. No interviews with suspension engineers, just "The Relentless Pursuit of Perfection."

Of course, you must decide, because you don't want your One Thing to be just anything!

Decide One Thing. Align Everything. Win!

- Why is making the differentiation decision so difficult?

- Consider some other iconic brands. Can you identify their One Thing?

- How long did it take these organizations to become iconic brands?

JOB ONE

For seventeen years, Ford used the tagline "Quality is Job One."

Ford had the courage to admit that their cars did indeed have quality problems, and fixing those problems was critical to the company's survival.

So critical that Ford made it Job One.

Ford also knew that they could not fix the quality problems without the help of their employees. Therefore, their global advertising campaign was designed to reach both consumers and employees.

The advertising helped employees understand the magnitude of the problem. Every night on TV.

Other elements of the change program engaged the employees in the process.

Eventually, the advertising even highlighted those employees who had signed up to be part of the solution. They went from factory workers to TV stars.

The campaign worked. Quality did indeed improve.

However, Ford abandoned the "Quality is Job One" tagline, and the company now ranks 27th (out of 34) in the J. D. Power and Associates 2012 U.S. Initial Quality Study.

This is a great case study in the difficulty of becoming differentiatingly great.

Perhaps Ford threw in the towel in frustration.

Perhaps the key stakeholders never really bought in.

Perhaps it was just an advertising campaign after all.

But the lesson is clear: only One Thing can be Job One.

Decide One Thing. Align Everything. Win!

- What is Job One for your organization?

- Do all of your customers and employees know exactly what it is?

- Do you have the organizational discipline to stay with it as long as it takes?

THE ONE HUNDRED MILLION
DOLLAR QUESTION

Another way to understand the One Thing is "The One Hundred Million Dollar Question." It goes like this.

"If we gave you $100 million to invest in your business with only one condition—that you had to invest all of the money in just one area—where would you invest it?"

You'd be surprised how many executive teams can't answer this question.

Obviously, there are a lot of things that you can do with $100M. We can see executive teams trying to avoid making a decision.

Often, they reply by saying that they would invest the $100M in three things.

Our response? "No. You can't have the money unless you invest all of it in just one area. I don't care what it is, but you are not allowed to dribble it out into three things … or twenty-seven things. Just One Thing."

The point of the question is to reinforce the idea that it is extremely difficult to become great at something, but it is impossible to become differentiatingly great at everything.

To become differentiatingly great at something, you must invest a disproportionate share of the organization's resources (money, people, and time) in it. Which means that you must invest less in other areas.

For example, Apple chose product design, specifically the user interface, as their One Thing. After decades of investment, they are indeed differentiatingly great.

This takes intense discipline. You will have to say no to a lot of good ideas in order to say yes to the best ones. You will have to stay focused on One Thing for a really long time. Perhaps decades.

Eventually, you will climb the ladder and create a brand that stands alone. Just like Apple.

Remember, it is better to be differentiatingly great at One Thing than disappointingly mediocre at dozens of things.

Decide One Thing. Align Everything. Win!

- Where would you invest the $100M?

- Are you tempted to say "three things"?

- How long does it take for organizations to become differentiatingly great?

THE ONE THING AND
THE HEDGEHOG

Jim Collins introduced the Hedgehog Concept in his landmark book, *Good to Great* (2001).

The Decide One Thing idea evolved from our work with high-growth organizations, many of which struggled to make the Hedgehog Concept work.

Collins developed the Hedgehog Concept for Fortune 500 companies, and described it as a "coherent concept" and a "unifying theme."

The Hedgehog "three circles" process was based on a Venn diagram with three circles: Economic Engine + Passion + Best in the World. An organization's Hedgehog was in the overlap of the Venn—a great concept.

Sadly, Collins reported that the average company took four years to discover their Hedgehog, and it took two more years for the Hedgehog to produce results.

That's a total of six years!

In contrast, the Decide One Thing process is for Fast Lane Leaders who want to accelerate results…and fast!

The Hedgehog was primarily an inwardly focused activity. In contrast, the Decide One Thing process is more externally focused, and is designed to identify your defining differentiation.

This defining differentiation is translated into a customer value proposition that can win new business and improve margins.

Many of our clients have completed the Decide One Thing process in 90 days.

That's 2,100 days faster than Good to Great.

Of course, the Decide One Thing process is the starting point, not the finish line. It can take another year—or more—to align everything. And becoming differentiatingly great is a lifelong quest.

Decide One Thing. Align Everything. Win!

- Has your organization attempted to apply the Hedgehog Concept?

- Were you ever able to definitively identify your Hedgehog?

- Did your Hedgehog generate results?

ONE TENTH OF ONE PERCENT

According to Wikipedia, 99.9 percent of human DNA is common to all human beings. Imagine—there are seven billion people of all shapes, sizes, heights, weights, sexes, and colors on the planet—and our DNA is 99.9 percent alike.

Thus, only one tenth of one percent of the DNA sequence is unique to each individual.

One tenth of one percent!

Organizations are the same—they are 99.9 percent alike. They all have accounting departments, websites, sales targets, press releases, pithy brochures, and golf balls with their company logo.

However, like the uniqueness in human DNA, your organization's defining differentiation will come from the 0.1 percent that makes you unique, such as:

- A unique component of your service delivery process.

- A unique aspect of your organization's worldview.

- A unique ingredient in your "special sauce."

- A unique asset, strength, or capability.

Like the scientists researching DNA, you might have to look at your organization under a microscope to find it.

For example, drive a BMW and a Lexus back-to-back. At first they will seem very similar. Nice-looking cars. Well appointed. Four doors. Four tires. Four cupholders.

On closer inspection, the differences will emerge. The BMW has a throatier exhaust note. The Lexus is quieter. The BMW's seats are more form-fitting, designed to hold you stable at the Nürburgring. The BMW will have touches of Alcantara, the suede-like material found in race cars. The Lexus will have plusher seats and softer refinements.

Each company has found their unique DNA. The difference may be just one tenth of one percent, but it is there.

The Decide One Thing process is one of discovery, exploration, and examination. It works best when the executive team embraces it as a top priority.

Decide One Thing. Align Everything. Win!

- What is your "one tenth of one percent"?

- Does your brand identity reflect your uniqueness?

- Does your organization stand out in the "sea of sameness"?

TRIATHLONS

Awhile back, a CEO asked me a very interesting question: "Can my One Thing be Three Things?"

My reflex reaction was to say, "Of course not."

However, as I thought about it, I used the following analogy with him: "Is being a triathlete a viable strategy for an athlete?"

The answer is "Yes, being a triathlete is viable. On one condition: you must *only* compete in triathlons."

The pure, specialist runner will beat the triathlete in a running race every time. The pure, specialist swimmer will beat the triathlete in a swimming race every time. The pure, specialist biker will beat the triathlete in a bike race every time.

But the triathlete will beat all of them in a triathlon.

As it turned out, the CEO was an accomplished triathlete. Thus, the analogy worked perfectly.

So it is a viable strategy to combine three things (or more) into your One Thing. McDonald's famous "special sauce" is a combination of multiple ingredients.

For example, we had a client who combined people, technology, and practices in a unique way. The three capabilities were so integrated and intertwined that they were essentially inseparable.

Almost Trinitarian.

Many organizations try to wiggle out of Deciding One Thing by using this concept.

"Our One Thing is Three Things."

But they miss the point. A triathlon really is just One Thing.

Remember, this differentiation strategy only works if your three things are so integrated that they really are One Thing. And you must only compete in markets where your "Three In One" Thing matches the customers' buying criteria. Your target customers must value your unique combination more than they value "point" solutions from other vendors.

Decide One Thing. Align Everything. Win!

- Is your One Thing a combination of three things?

- How do you uniquely combine three things into One?

- Are you only entering races where your "Three in One" Thing gives you a competitive advantage?

CHAPTER THREE

EXAMPLES AND CASE STUDIES

SOME OF OUR EXAMPLES ARE WELL-KNOWN
BRANDS. OTHERS ARE SMALL COMPANIES
THAT YOU HAVE NEVER HEARD OF.
TOGETHER, THEY PROVE THAT THE
DECIDE ONE THING CONCEPT WORKS.

GOING GAGA

There are millions of singers in the world.

But there is only One Lady Gaga.

You probably won't be surprised to learn that I am not a big Lady Gaga fan, but I have to give her credit—she definitely is unique.

Every organization would be lucky to have such a unique brand identity and market position. Most wallow in a drab sea of sameness.

Breaking into any new industry is hard. But breaking into the entertainment industry must be the hardest of them all. There are literally millions of singers, dancers, and entertainers vying to become the next big thing.

Stefani Germanotta was just another singer in New York. Modestly talented. Hopelessly romantic. Totally undifferentiated.

Until she reinvented herself as Lady Gaga.

The Lady—as she is often called—is a profound example of the power of differentiation.

The Lady cultivates her brand with near-military rigor. From her 38 million (and growing) Twitter followers to her outlandish outfits that make every day look like Halloween, she has become a one-of-a-kind brand.

Immediately recognizable. Notoriously unignorable.

As a result, we are featuring Lady Gaga as our first case study. Clients ask, "How does an organization create a unique, defining, and differentiating identity?"

We simply reply by saying, "You do it by 'Going GaGa,' which is shorthand for 'Good at, Great at.'"

Lady Gaga is good at many things—she is a good singer, she is a good dancer, she is good (but not great) looking. But she is differentiatingly great at being different!

Decide One Thing. Align Everything. Win!

- Is being different your One Thing?

- If so, how can you go from bland and vanilla to notoriously unignorable?

- What will it take to develop and cultivate your brand with near-military rigor?

WE ONLY MAKE ONE THING

There are a dozen car companies competing in the premium luxury segment.

But there is only One "Ultimate Driving Machine."

BMW began using the tagline "The Ultimate Driving Machine" in 1975. Recently, however, they moved in a different direction, with the ill-fated "JOY" campaign.

Happy cars. Happy people. Happy life. Yuck!

Thankfully, BMW is set to revive The Ultimate Driving Machine tagline with a new commercial. Here is the text:

We don't make sports cars. We don't make SUVs. We don't make hybrids, and we don't make luxury sedans. We only make one thing, The Ultimate Driving Machine.

Imagine the internal debates at BMW.

The VP of quality, who argued that the campaign should highlight BMW's quality, which is on par with Lexus. Or the VP of design, who argued that the campaign should highlight the car's unique styling. Or the VP of engineering, who argued that the campaign should explain all of the sophisticated technology.

Kudos to BMW for reviving one of the greatest campaigns ever. And for having the discipline to stay intensely focused on their One Thing.

BMW is indeed good at many things—quality, design, engineering, and more. All of these are important to succeeding in the luxury car segment. But BMW is differentiatingly great at creating a high-performance driving experience.

That's why they are The Ultimate Driving Machine.

Decide One Thing. Align Everything. Win!

- Is high performance the One Thing that you do best?

- If so, what would it take to become differentiatingly great—significantly better than any other competitor?

- Are your customers really willing to pay a premium for superior performance?

FERRARI IN THE CITY
WITH NO ROADS

There are dozens of sports cars.

But only One captures the heart like a Ferrari.

The city of Venice is an amazing place.

It has no roads and no cars, but it does have a Ferrari store. This is a real tribute to the power of the Ferrari brand.

The city with no roads and no cars has a Ferrari store!

The store's prominent feature is a red (of course) Ferrari Formula 1 car on display. The store sells T-shirts starting at forty euros, scale models of Ferrari cars, Ferrari sneakers, Ferrari hats, Ferrari luggage, Ferrari gloves, Ferrari pens, Ferrari sunglasses, Ferrari flags, and more.

There is even a children's section that sells Ferrari onesies, Ferrari baby shoes, and all sorts of other items to indoctrinate your child into the faithful.

I happened to be there on the weekend of the Formula 1 race at Monza, Italy—the home of Ferrari. The Ferrari Scuderia (Italian for "stable") won the race, and the entire nation wildly celebrated.

Very few brands achieve iconic status. Fewer still achieve the kind of fanatical evangelicalism among their customers that Ferrari does.

The Ferrari brand and image have been carefully cultivated through incredible discipline, or what we call "brand cohesion." Some of the key elements of the Ferrari brand include a design aesthetic that makes their cars look like 220-MPH pieces of art, an obsession with the color red, and a legacy of racing championships.

All infused with a flair that is uniquely Italian.

Ferrari is good at many things—engineering, design, branding, and more. But they are differentiatingly great at making people lust after inanimate objects.

Decide One Thing. Align Everything. Win!

- Is creating cool, sexy products the One Thing that you do best?

- If so, what will it take to become differentiatingly great—significantly better than any other competitor?

- What percentage of the market is willing to pay a premium for your superior products?

EXTREMELY EXTREME

There are thousands of canned soft drinks.

But there is only One that "Gives You Wings."

Austrian entrepreneur Dietrich Mateschitz founded Red Bull in 1984, two years after experiencing the effects of Asian "tonic drinks" at a bar in the Mandarin Hotel in Hong Kong.

Like many other great differentiators, Red Bull was not just a new company with a new product.

In fact, Red Bull created a totally new product category, and now dominates the category they created. They are the number one energy drink in the world.

Their drinks, sold in small silver cans, contain caffeine, taurine, B-group vitamins, sucrose, and glucose. According to the company, since 1987 around 30 billion cans of Red Bull have been consumed—more than 4.6 billion in 2011.

Red Bull has used extreme sports and extreme sports athletes to build an amazingly powerful brand. The company sponsors cliff diving, acrobatic free running, kiteboarding, windsurfing, rock climbing, and more.

In fact, a Red Bull-sponsored BASE jumper even flew a wingsuit (complete with Red Bull logo) from the top of the Himalayas.

The lesson for all executive teams is this: in every market—and for every value proposition—there is great opportunity at the extremes.

Skull Candy is the Red Bull of headphones. Loudmouth is the Red Bull of golf clothing. Lamborghini is the Red Bull of performance cars.

Sometimes it is better to SHOUT OUT at the extremes than blend into the boring middle.

Red Bull is good at many things—the product tastes good, gives you a good buzz, and is reasonably priced. But Red Bull is differentiatingly great at leveraging extreme sports to dominate the energy drink market.

Decide One Thing. Align Everything. Win!

- Is "being extreme" the One Thing that you do best?

- If so, what will it take to become differentiatingly great—significantly better than any other competitor?

- What percentage of your customers will resonate with the extreme message?

RETURNING TIRES

There are thousands of retailers.

But only One will let you return products that they don't even sell.

There is a legendary story at Nordstrom about a customer who came into a brand-new store in Alaska to return two truck tires. The sales clerk accepted the return, even though Nordstrom has never sold tires.

Can you imagine refunding money to a customer for a product that you never sold?

As the story goes, the customer did indeed buy a tire from a store at that location, but that was before Nordstrom moved in. (The location had been previously occupied by Northern Commercial of Alaska. They sold an eclectic mix of goods, from towels and linens to automotive supplies.)

Rather than fight with the customer—creating an enemy for life—the sales clerk accepted the return, and created a customer for life.

Let's do the math.

The lifetime value of a Nordstrom customer is in the tens of thousands of dollars. The value of an incredibly satisfied customer who tells everyone he knows how great you are is worth hundreds of thousands.

The value of a legendary story is worth millions. (Every Nordstrom employee and millions of consumers know "The Tire Story.")

So the sales clerk—empowered by Nordstrom management to do the right thing—gives a customer roughly $100 for two old tires. The gesture returns millions of dollars in business and goodwill.

In contrast, I'm not sure the auto parts store that sold the guy the tires in the first place would have given him his money back. The clerk probably would have pointed to some sign taped to the wall and mumbled about their thirty-day return policy.

Nordstrom has nice products, nice stores, and fair prices. But they are differentiatingly great at serving their customers. Their return policy is just one example of how they have aligned every aspect of their organization with their One Thing.

Decide One Thing. Align Everything. Win!

- Is customer service the One Thing that you do best?

- If so, what will it take to become differentiatingly great—significantly better than any other competitor?

- Do your service policies empower front-line people to do the right thing, no questions asked?

CRAZY EDDIE

There are thousands of retailers.

But there was only One Crazy Eddie.

Back in the '70s and '80s, a New York electronics retailer called Crazy Eddie became famous for an advertising slogan based on their aggressively low prices.

"Crazy Eddie: his prices are INSAAAAANE!"

(As it turns out, low price was not their One Thing; fraud was. The founders were charged with fraud and money laundering, and eventually spent time in jail.)

However, the story is a good reminder that there is a Crazy Eddie in every market segment.

Crazy Eddie is representative of the company that decides that rock-bottom price is the way to gain market share. Sometimes, their behavior is simply irrational.

Otherwise known as crazy!

However, in every market, there is a group of customers whose dominant buying motive is price. Above all, these customers want to save money, and are willing to sacrifice other things, such as convenience, features, or even quality, to do so.

As a result, in every market, there is a company with a business model that is optimized to profitably serve the low-price segment. They are obsessive about cost control, supply chain management, and purchasing.

These things allow them to compete at price points that competitors can't match.

So as you consider which One Thing is best for you, don't categorically rule out price. Tangible value propositions, like cost savings, are far easier to sell than intangibles like superior service.

Who knows? Maybe you'll be the Crazy Eddie of your market—without the fraud, of course.

Decide One Thing. Align Everything. Win!

- Is competing on price the One Thing that you do best?

- If so, what will it take to become differentiatingly great—significantly better than any other competitor?

- If it is not you, who is the Crazy Eddie in your market? How can you beat them?

RELENTLESSLY PROACTIVE

There are hundreds of construction companies.

But there is only One that is "Relentlessly Proactive."

The commercial interior construction industry is brutally competitive. With the downturn in the economy, the competition became cutthroat. Companies were quoting crazy prices in desperate attempts to survive.

In addition, project timelines have been slashed to accelerate move-in dates and save money. What was once a twenty-week project is now a twelve-week rush job.

To compete in this new world, Bognet Construction built their differentiation around the concept of being Relentlessly Proactive.

This is an example of taking one aspect of customer service and optimizing your business model around it.

This differentiation—like that of many organizations— was rooted in the behavior and beliefs of the organization's founder. Jim Bognet personifies what it means to be Relentlessly Proactive.

Bognet's philosophy is that people hate surprises. So everyone works tirelessly to anticipate things that might go wrong or delay a project.

Bognet developed proprietary tools and methodologies which enable them to be Relentlessly Proactive. These tools transcend every aspect of their business—from estimating to project management to accounting.

In addition, Bognet only hires Relentlessly Proactive people. Highly qualified people who are not Relentlessly Proactive don't make the cut.

Bognet is good at many things—project management, estimating, engineering, and more. But their Relentlessly Proactive behavior is what differentiates them from the competition.

Relentlessly Proactive is more than a tagline. For Bognet Construction, it defines who they are and how they win.

Decide One Thing. Align Everything. Win!

- Is there a specific aspect of customer service that is the One Thing that you do best?

- If so, what will it take to become differentiatingly great—significantly better than any other competitor?

- Do your customers expect both great service and the lowest price?

THE RIGHT ANSWER

There are hundreds of government contractors.

But there is only One that helps clients find "The Right Answer."

Group W was founded by five colleagues who had experienced what they described as "the lameness and creativity-sapping mediocrity" of traditional government contracting firms.

They started Group W with a radically different vision and plan to do things the right way.

Group W's clients are some of the most demanding in the world. They are tackling some of the world's most complex questions. Questions that really matter.

Group W's goal is to help their clients find the right answer. The answer that really works.

Finding the right answer requires Group W to forge a unique partnership with what they call "visionary clients."

For this partnership to produce results, Group W must recruit and deploy exceptional people who possess a unique combination of skills.

And since the phrase "exceptional people" has the potential for a wide range of interpretations, it was

63

important for Group W's leaders to clarify exactly what they meant.

Group W has a unique perspective on the characteristics that make someone exceptional, shaped by the specific requirements of the work and by the unconventional aspects of their culture.

The Group W culture was designed to foster the kind of unconventional, free thinking required to find The Right Answer to their clients' most complex questions. They have even taken the time to write their unique culture in a fascinating document called, "The Cultural Manifesto."

Group W is good at many things—statistical analysis, modeling, software development, and more. But they are differentiatingly great at solving complex problems that traditional firms can't solve.

That's why they are The Right Answer.

Decide One Thing. Align Everything. Win!

- Is solving unsolvable problems the One Thing that you do best?

- If so, what will it take to become differentiatingly great—significantly better than any other competitor?

- What kind of culture do you need to create in order to enable differentiating greatness?

PRODUCING FRUIT

There are hundreds of firms that build websites.

But there is only One that helps churches "produce fruit."

For every organization, websites are important.

But for churches, websites have eternally significant consequences.

Brad Hill is an Internet pioneer who founded Site-Organic to help churches and ministries build websites and take their ministries online. Translated into ministry language, this means that the website must produce fruit, such as:

- Building community among the congregation, leading to increased retention.

- Communicating the Gospel to unbelievers, leading to their conversion.

- Distributing content to all, leading to their spiritual growth.

- Providing state-of-the-art tools to the staff, leading to improved productivity.

So, what does it take for a website to produce this kind of fruit?

Great design is important, but not enough. A sophisticated content management system is important, but again not enough. Great technology is important, but technology alone will not produce fruit.

Therefore, SiteOrganic decided that their One Thing would be their unique blend of great design, a great platform, great tools, great support, great people, new technologies, and best practices.

We came to refer to this as the Organic Blend.

SiteOrganic is good at many things—design, platforms, tools, support, and more. But they are differentiatingly great at blending all of those things into websites that produce fruit.

Decide One Thing. Align Everything. Win!

- Is your One Thing the result of a unique, one-of-a-kind blend of capabilities?

- If so, what will it take to become differentiatingly great—significantly better than any other competitor?

- Can you translate that blend into a compelling value proposition?

DEVELOPING ULTIMATE TEAMMATES

There are thousands of leaders who say that people are their greatest asset.

But there is only One that is "Developing Ultimate Teammates."

BTI360 is a software development firm that works with government clients.

Growth had plateaued, and they were struggling to articulate what set them apart from the hundreds of other software companies in the Washington, DC, area. A committee had spent months working through Jim Collins's Hedgehog Concept, but they never broke the code.

In addition, competing in the government sector meant that they had multiple stakeholders. The specific government client. The prime contractor. The employee.

I was having lunch with MJ Wivell and Jeremy Nimtz, discussing their One Thing, and asked them a question that was the turning point in the process.

"What would you do for free?"

For some organizations, their One Thing is rooted in a deep-seated passion. This was reflected in their answer.

For the founders of BTI360, their passion is to develop people and help them grow. And they are not just concerned with helping people grow in their careers; they want to help people grow in their personal lives as well.

Thus, BTI360 decided to make the employees* (and potential employees) their primary focus. To ensure that they attracted the right people, BTI360 created an amazing recruiting and on-boarding process.

BTI360 is good at many things—software technology, Agile development, KANBAN, and more. But they are differentiatingly great at developing people, and that's why they win.

Decide One Thing. Align Everything. Win!

- Is developing people the One Thing that you do best?

- If so, what will it take to become differentiatingly great—significantly better than any other competitor?

- What would you do for free?

* BTI360 calls people Teammates, not employees, which is exactly what you would expect from an organization that puts people first.

SIGNATURE STYLE

There are dozens of companies that distribute kitchen cabinets to homebuilders.

But there is only One that helps builders create their own unique Signature Style.

Signature is a distributor of kitchen cabinets and stairs, serving builders in the Washington, DC, area.

Their customers—medium-sized homebuilders—were under increasing pressure to differentiate their homes.

And one of the best ways to wow a customer is with a "wow" kitchen.

But how do you create a "wow" kitchen if every builder has the same cabinets?

For Signature, the answer would come from a most unusual place.

Signature owned a low-volume manufacturing plant. At first, the plant was just used to make replacement doors for cabinets that had been damaged. (Its primary purpose was to manufacture Signature's line of stairs.)

However, Signature began to design and manufacture unique kitchen pieces, such as special range hoods or customized corner cabinets, for some of their builders. These unique pieces were combined with the standard kitchen cabinet products to create a one-of-a-kind kitchen.

This process helped their customers create a unique "Signature Style," which differentiates them from other builders.

Being realists, Signature's leaders, brothers John and Chris Lombardozzi, would never have said that manufacturing was their greatest strength.

But while manufacturing was not their greatest strength, it was their most unique asset.

Signature is good at many things—kitchen design, installation, and indeed manufacturing. But they are differentiatingly great at combining standard cabinets with custom-designed pieces, thus helping their customers find their own Signature Style.

Decide One Thing. Align Everything. Win!

- Do you own any unique assets that are potentially the source of your differentiation?

- Can you combine your unique assets and strengths in a way that makes them your One Thing?

- Can you do so in a way that is truly differentiating and significantly better than the competition?

NEVER LOSE SUCTION

There are dozens of companies that make vacuum cleaners, and there are thousands of different models.

But there is only One that doesn't lose suction.

The story of Dyson is a testament to the irrational perseverance required to become differentiatingly great at something.

It took James Dyson five years and 5,127 prototypes to perfect the Dual Cyclone™ technology that is at the core of the Dyson vacuum.

According to Dyson's Website, "New ideas are the lifeblood of Dyson. Every year, we invest our profits back into harnessing them at our research and development laboratory in Wiltshire, UK. There are 650 engineers and scientists based there. Thinking, testing, breaking, questioning."

Thinking. Testing. Breaking. Questioning. These sound like words you would use to describe the process of curing cancer, not cleaning carpet.

Dyson's passion for design and innovation is inspiring. Their vacuums are so cool that even guys drool over the designs. Of course, the vacuums are sold at a premium price, often as much as 50% higher than "comparable" machines.

The $650 DC28 model even includes "Airmuscle™ technology," which pushes the cleaner head deeper into the carpet to remove embedded dirt and pet hair.

Who wouldn't want a vacuum with Airmuscle technology?

I'm sure people told James Dyson that it was impossible to make a vacuum into a high-priced fashion accessory that people would pay a premium for.

James Dyson—driven to prove people wrong—refused to listen. Perhaps that is why he is now Sir James Dyson, appointed to the rank of Knight Bachelor in 2007.

Dyson is good at many things—engineering, industrial design, marketing, and more. But they are differentiatingly great at reinventing stale product categories with breakthrough designs.

Decide One Thing. Align Everything. Win!

- Is innovation the One Thing that you do best?

- If so, what will it take to become differentiatingly great—significantly better than any other competitor?

- If so, can you invent a killer feature such as "never losing suction"?

YES, SIR!

There are thousands of companies that sell financial services.

But there is only One that calls you "Sir!"

USAA was started in 1922, when twenty-five army officers in San Antonio, TX, agreed to insure each other's cars when no one else would.

Today, USAA offers a full range of financial products to millions of members, all of whom have served in the military or are family members of someone who has served.

When you call the company's 800 number, a real person answers the phone. Normally on the first ring. That person treats you with dignity, honor, and respect.

The employees even call you "Sir!"

USAA's One Thing is serving a unique customer demographic. They have spent almost one hundred years building institutional knowledge, customized products, and exceptional service.

They are indeed differentiatingly great at serving the military, and according to a recent company survey, 95 percent of their customers intend to be "customers for life."

Many, like yours truly, are members of a family that are multigenerational USAA members.

Of course, some would argue that USAA could grow their business by offering services to other demographics. But even the company's organizational structure is designed to be distinctive. As they say, "USAA is not a publicly traded company, so we don't answer to stockholders—we answer to our members."

And diversification would water down their distinctiveness.

USAA is good at many things—investment management, insurance, customer service, and more. But they are differentiatingly great at serving a unique—and most deserving—demographic.

Decide One Thing. Align Everything. Win!

- Is serving a unique demographic the One Thing that you do best?

- If so, what will it take to become differentiatingly great—significantly better than any other competitor?

- Do you have the organizational discipline to say no to opportunities that would distract you?

THE BIG THINKERS THINK TANK

There are hundreds of think tanks in the world.

But there is only One that integrates the entire conservative worldview into a visionary agenda.

The Heritage Foundation is a conservative think tank with an extremely broad range of policy expertise.

Although they are a think tank—complete with posh offices just minutes from the White House and the halls of Congress—they refer to themselves as "policy entrepreneurs."

The Heritage mission is to "formulate and promote conservative public policies based on the principles of free enterprise, limited government, individual freedom, traditional American values, and a strong national defense."

(In contrast, many other think tanks specialize in just one issue, such as national defense.)

In April 2007, led by their visionary CEO, Dr. Edwin Feulner, and his right-hand COO, Phil Truluck, The Heritage Foundation undertook a ten-year campaign that integrated ten specific policy areas into a holistic and visionary agenda.

They call it "Leadership for America–Ten Transformational Initiatives," and Heritage is the only organization with the breadth and depth to be able to lead the charge.

You may not agree with their ideology, but The Heritage Foundation is a great example of how a nonprofit can leverage One Thing to make a huge impact.

They are also a good illustration of how every industry has one organization with the product breadth and vision to be the integrated solutions architect.

Heritage is good at many things—conducting research, writing papers, providing talking points on specific policy issues, and more. But they are differentiatingly great at integrating the entire conservative worldview into a visionary agenda.

Decide One Thing. Align Everything. Win!

- Is providing an "integrated solution" the One Thing that you do best?

- If so, what will it take to become differentiatingly great—significantly better than any other competitor?

- Do you really have all the pieces required?

SO WHAT?

There are millions of churches in the world.

But there is only One that answers the question, "So what?"

Senior Pastor Lon Solomon of McLean Bible Church in McLean, VA, began using the question "So what?" near the end of his sermons back in the 1980s.

He's been saying it without fail in every sermon for nearly three decades!

He now prompts his 15,000-person congregation to shout out the question by saying, "Now it is time to answer our most important question. And you all know what it is. C'mon now…one…two…three…"

And the audience shouts out, "SO WHAT?"

Lon started doing this as a way to connect with an increasingly secularized and biblically illiterate popula-tion. As he often says, "People don't think church and the Bible are bad, they just think they are irrelevant."

The moral of the story is that every organization—even churches—needs a defining differentiation.

Some churches focus on the poor. Others focus on missions. Others on discipleship. However, since every ministry idea is inherently good, most churches have difficulty focusing and suffer from the "all things to all people" problem.

Since MBC is focused on communicating biblical information in a relevant way, they don't use big, scary words, like "propitiation" or "sanctification." They don't sing four-hundred-year-old songs in Latin.

McLean Bible Church is good at many things—children's ministry, adult education, worship music, and more. But they are differentiatingly great at communicating biblical information in a relevant way.

As a result, they do indeed answer the "most important question—So what?"

Decide One Thing. Align Everything. Win!

- Is communicating in a clear and relevant way the One Thing that you do best?

- If so, what will it take to become differentiatingly great—significantly better than any other competitor?

- Are there people who think that your products or services are irrelevant?

GROW AHEAD...

There are hundreds of accounting, human resources, and technology firms.

But there is only One that provides integrated back-office solutions to help clients grow.

Michael Tinsley founded NeoSystems Corp. in 2000 to provide accounting services to government contractors.

The NeoSystems name was chosen to reflect Michael's bold vision of a company that would revolutionize the accounting industry, creating a new category of professional services firms.

As the company grew, they developed a new strategy to expand beyond the core managed accounting services business. This involved adding human resources and information technology services.

The idea is to revolutionize these three sectors by combining them into one integrated, strategic back office.

The vision came to be illustrated by a Venn diagram with three circles, representing accounting, HR, and IT.

The Venn diagram—used to graphically convey their One Thing—drove a complete brand overhaul and brought all of the messaging into alignment with the new strategy.

A new tagline, "Grow Ahead...We've Got Your Back Office," also translated NeoSystem's One Thing into a compelling value proposition.

NeoSystems created new service offerings, new core values, new proposal language, a new organizational structure, a new performance management system, a new dashboard, new job descriptions, a new website, and more.

Each of these individual changes had an impact...but the cumulative effect of all of them together has been a stunning transformation.

NeoSystems is good at many things—accounting, financial planning, contract management, payroll, and IT. But they are differentiatingly great at integrating all of them into a strategic back office.

Decide One Thing. Align Everything. Win!

- Is your One Thing the result of a unique combination of three things?

- If so, what will it take to become differentiatingly great—better than any other competitor?

- Are customers in your market willing to pay a premium for that integration?

BE SQUARE

There are millions of restaurants that serve hamburgers.

But only One makes them square.

Differentiation is essential to survive in brutally competitive markets like fast food.

Wendy's has square burgers, which makes them stand out. They are square for a reason. As Wendy's founder Dave Thomas used to say, "Our burgers are square because we don't cut corners on quality."

But their real differentiation is freshness.

"At Wendy's, everything we do spins off one word—FRESH."

My wife Twee used to work at Wendy's. (As part of her job, she actually dressed up as Wendy to attend community events. Twee is Vietnamese, so you can imagine the sight of her in a red wig, striped bloomers, and freckles!)

As a result of her experience, I still get the full sales pitch every time we eat at Wendy's. She extols the virtues of fresh hamburger, fresh tomatoes, fresh onions and fresh chili. She tells stories of slicing fresh tomatoes and onions every morning.

Giant crates of real heads of lettuce arrive every morning—not shredded green stuff in big bags.

Ground beef comes in a bag and is freshly formed into patties every morning. (McDonald's ships their burgers frozen.)

Burgers are freshly cooked to order, not premade and wrapped ahead of time.

Wendy's was also the first of the big three hamburger franchises to have a salad bar.

Wendy's is good at many things—speed, menu choices, restaurant decor, and more. But they are differentiatingly great at freshness. So if freshness is your dominant buying motive, there is only one choice.

Decide One Thing. Align Everything. Win!

- Is there some small thing that you can make your One Thing?

- If so, what will it take to become differentiatingly great—significantly better than any other competitor?

- Can you bring it to life with some unique branding idea, such as square burgers?

THE RELENTLESS PURSUIT

The premium car market has many great competitors, including BMW, Mercedes, Audi, Cadillac, Jaguar, and more.

But there is only One driven by "The Relentless Pursuit of Perfection."

Toyota decided to move upscale, and wisely created a new brand to do so. Lexus was launched in the United States in 1989.

But imagine the competitive challenge of entering the premium automobile market. There are extremely strong and very established competitors. Many of which have been making cars since the car was invented.

Lexus cars are now sold globally, and they are Japan's largest-selling premium brand. They are also a fantastic illustration of the Decide One Thing … Align Everything … Win model.

Lexus chose quality as their One Thing, but set for themselves the highest possible standard: perfection.

Of course, when your promise is perfection, customers will hold you to it. I'm sure many a customer has thrown a problem back in Lexus's face with some sarcastic quip. "Perfect—yeah right!"

But Lexus properly understood that the quest for perfection—like the quest for differentiating greatness—would not be easy. They would have to be relentless in the pursuit.

Early Lexus commercials showed ball bearings rolling perfectly along perfectly aligned seams. That image highlighted the obsessive detail of the motor mounts, designed to reduce engine vibration.

Unlike Ford, Lexus truly made quality "Job One," and the brand is routinely in first place in the J. D. Power quality rankings.

Lexus is good at many things—design, performance, service, and more. But they are differentiatingly great at defining and delivering perfection.

Decide One Thing. Align Everything. Win!

- Is quality your One Thing?

- If so, what will it take to become differentiatingly great—maybe even perfect?

- What recovery mechanisms will you need to build for times when you fall short of delivering the perfection you promised?

GAMECHANGERS. GUARANTEED.

There are thousands of executive search firms.

But only one delivers GameChangers. Guaranteed.

In today's turbulent environment, organizations face unprecedented challenges. Meeting those challenges requires senior executives who are GameChangers.

GameChangers are rare and difficult to find. Just because an executive has been a top performer does not mean that they are a GameChanger and can get the job done in a new company's culture.

In addition, not all GameChangers are alike. For example, the skills and experiences required to lead a start-up through an IPO are very different from those required to turnaround an underperforming division.

Top Gun Ventures, founded by Don Tuttle and Pete Donovan, is a very unique executive search firm that specializes in finding GameChangers for their clients.

From the beginning, Don and Pete were intent on changing the game in the executive search business. "The traditional Executive Search process is broken" is one of Don's favorite lines and Pete observes "there is 'no accountability' by traditional search firms that their candidate will attain the long term goals they were hired for."

Their model starts with the unique partners in the firm, all of whom have extensive executive experience. Their motto is, "It takes a GameChanger to find a GameChanger."

In addition, they have developed unique and proprietary processes that allow them to find and recruit the right GameChanger for the job. This starts with a taxonomy of the different kinds of GameChangers, which delineates the nuances between turnaround artists and high growth leaders.

Finally, Top Gun Ventures actually guarantees that their candidate will deliver the results they were hired to achieve.

Top Gun Ventures is good at many things, but they are differentiatingly great at finding GameChangers, and that is why they win.

Decide One Thing. Align Everything. Win!

- Is the traditional business model in your industry totally broken?

- Is there an opportunity for your organization to be a GameChanger in your industry?

- Are you confident enough in your value proposition that you will guarantee results?

CHAPTER FOUR

THE DECISION MAKERS

YOU MUST DECIDE WHO WILL DECIDE.

THE ONE JOB DESCRIPTION
THAT'S MISSING

Virtually every employee on the planet has a job description. (The description may be wrong or outdated, but somewhere in the HR files, one exists.)

But the one job description that is missing is the job description for the executive team.

Most executive teams simply meet once a month and bombard each other with PowerPoint slides. (In most of the executive meetings I attend, the only one paying attention to what is being said is the person who is speaking. Virtually everyone else is doodling, texting, multitasking, or dozing off.)

Is presenting slides to each other really the best use of executive talent?

Not really.

Executives are strategists and problem solvers, so the best use of their time is for them to work together solving the organization's most pressing problems.

So the job description of the executive team should include:

- Deciding which One Thing will be organization's defining differentiation.

- Creating a strong and unifying corporate identity.

- Designing a winning corporate strategy.

- Developing the talent strategy to attract, develop, reward, and unleash the very best people.

- Building the management system to align resources and optimize performance.

But the starting point—and most important deliverable—is the organization's defining differentiation.

One of the unintended byproducts of the Decide One Thing process is improved executive teamwork. Done properly, the process forces executives to work together and identify the One Thing that everyone in the organization can rally around.

Decide One Thing. Align Everything. Win!

- Does your executive team have a job description, complete with specific deliverables and goals?

- Do your executive meetings effectively leverage the strategic problem-solving skills of the team?

- If your employees gave the executive team a performance review, what would it say?

DECIDING ONE THING
IS A HARD THING

Executives are paid to make decisions, so why have few organizations decided their One Thing?

Because deciding One Thing is a hard thing!

Frankly, this process would be a lot easier if we advised organizations to pick three things. But it would be a lot less effective.

Executives struggle to pick just One Thing as their defining differentiation.

As one lamented, "What if we pick the wrong thing?"

It is true that if the executive team does not get this right, the whole organization will underperform.

In addition, most executive teams fear that not every customer will value their One Thing.

And indeed, that is exactly what will happen.

But that is not all that will happen.

You will win lots of customers who do value your One Thing.

Because your value proposition is clear, you will attract the right customers. Since they value your One Thing, they will pay you for it. (Analyze your profitability on a customer-by-customer level, and you will certainly see that not all customers are created equal!)

Growth will accelerate. Profitability will improve. Win rates will go up. Retention will go up.

But making this decision requires strategic courage.

Yes, it is hard to Decide One Thing. And it is even harder to implement that decision. It requires unwavering commitment. Dogmatic discipline. Relentless focus.

Decide One Thing. Align Everything. Win!

- Does your executive team struggle to make big strategic decisions?

- Are you worried that you will pick the wrong thing?

- Do you buy the argument that you will repel customers who don't value your One Thing—but attract those who do?

STAKEHOLDERS

The senior executive team must Decide One Thing.

But they would be silly to do so without considering the key stakeholders.

For example, some of the key stakeholders who can help shape the decision include:

1. Investors and shareholders

2. Customers (we will cover them in a later chapter)

3. Employees, especially managers, high-potentials, and important influencers

4. Vendors and suppliers

5. Strategic partners

Obviously, when it comes to deciding on your defining differentiation, not all of these stakeholders have an equal impact.

Some executive teams feel that consulting a broad range of people during the process will slow things down.

In fact, the opposite is true.

Consulting with key stakeholders during the decision-making process does take time. But you more than make up for it during the implementation phase.

We all learned this lesson from the fable of the tortoise and the hare.

Stakeholders who have been consulted feel valued. They feel like they have been heard, even if the organization does not use their specific suggestions.

And since they feel a much greater sense of buy-in, they will become champions for the implementation.

Accelerating results.

Decide One Thing. Align Everything. Win!

- Who are the key stakeholders that should be consulted in your Decide One Thing process?

- How can you efficiently include them without things grinding to a halt?

- How do you deal with the doubters, detractors, and congenital naysayers?

DEBATE, DECIDE, AND ALIGN

One of the most dysfunctional and destructive organizational pathologies is undermining, especially at executive levels.

Unfortunately, we see this all the time.

Issues are discussed at the executive meeting. Alternatives are debated. And eventually, a decision about the best course of action is made.

Far too often, what happens next is that executives who did not get their way undermine the decision.

We call this pathology "Debate, Decide, and Undermine."

Sometimes the undermining is overt, blatant, and public, such as when an executive says, "They made a dumb decision."

Most of the time, however, the undermining is much more covert.

Whispering at the water cooler. Backstabbing in the bathroom. Sniping at Starbucks.

This kind of behavior, especially at executive levels, must never be tolerated.

We have seen a lot of organizations overlook this behavior because the executive was "making the numbers" or "has been with us from the beginning."

Don't fall for this line of reasoning.

Obviously, having a "debate, decide, and align" model is important for all key decisions.

But it is absolutely non-negotiable when it comes to the decision about your defining differentiation.

The executive team must be completely united.

Unequivocally unified.

When they come to a shift point, high-performance executive teams debate, decide, and align. Once a decision is made about the organization's One Thing, everyone must align behind it, even it if wasn't their idea.

Decide One Thing. Align Everything. Win!

- Does your executive team have vigorous debates?

- Is there freedom to "confront the brutal facts"?

- Does everyone align once a decision is made?

ALL FOR ONE (THING)

The Three Musketeers is a novel by Alexandre Dumas set in seventeenth-century Paris. It tells the story of a young man named d'Artagnan who wants to join the Musketeers of the Guard.

The Three Musketeers made the phrase "all for one, and one for all" famous (tous pour un, et un pour tous).

Like the Musketeers, executives must be "All for One… Thing."

In high-performance organizations, executives operate as One Team, working together to decide which One Thing will be their defining differentiation. Once the decision has been made, they continue working together to translate their One Thing into a sustainable competitive advantage.

To create an "All for One" executive team, high performers leverage a number of tools, including:

- Shared vision. Executives develop the long-term vision in a collaborative way that encourages buy-in.

- Shared values. Only executives who share (and model) the organization's values are on the team. Executives who "make the numbers" but undermine the values are invited to find employment elsewhere.

- Shared goals. There is one overall corporate goal that every executive is focused on achieving.

- Shared rewards. Every executive has a significant percentage of his or her compensation tied to overall corporate—not individual—goals.

- Shared experiences. In many organizations, executives simply don't spend any time together. Sometimes, a good off-site meeting can provide a relational foundation for teamwork.

- Rotational assignments. Walking a mile in another leader's moccasins can go a long way.

Aligning hard-charging and independent leaders into a cohesive team does not happen by itself. It takes real leadership and team-building from the CEO. You have to pull all of the alignment levers.

Decide One Thing. Align Everything. Win!

- Does your executive team model the "All for One" philosophy?

- Have you pulled all of the alignment levers?

- Are you tolerating executives who don't share your values?

CHAPTER FIVE

DEFINE YOUR MARKET

IT IS BETTER TO DOMINATE ONE MARKET
THAN DABBLE IN A DOZEN OF THEM.

ONE CORE MARKET

I've spent most of the last decade trying to get organizations to be more focused.

The One Thing concept originated from our work with a startup that raised almost $1 million of "friends and family" money. Flush with cash and unbridled bravado, they set out to conquer the world.

So far, so good.

All great startups have big dreams and bold visions.

However, this company decided to attack about a dozen different markets.

Their strategy was to build a social network that blew away Facebook.

And build a payment system that blew away Visa.

And build a contact management system that blew away Microsoft Outlook.

And revolutionize the trade show industry.

And revolutionize the singles club scene.

And become the hottest thing on college campuses.

And reinvent online advertising.

And more. All at once.

Although we advised them over and over to pick One Core Market and then Decide One Thing to become differentiatingly great at it, they never listened. As a result, the organization never generated market traction.

Their failure strengthened our resolve.

Decide One Thing. Align Everything. Win!

- How many markets are you pursuing?

- Are you diluting your resources and attention by doing too many things?

- Does dabbling ever win?

FOUR QUESTIONS

There are many ways to define your target market.

We use a simple four-question model.

This model allows organizations to define a market with the right level of clarity.

Here are the four questions:

- Who is your target customer?

- What do you sell them?

- Where do you operate?

- How much do you charge?

Thus, Who + What + Where + How Much = your One Core Market.

While these four questions may seem simple, many organizations struggle to answer them precisely.

And remember, our goal is to find a single, unifying, corporate-level differentiation. Thus, we want to define our market at a corporate level as well.

For example, a huge global corporation like BMW would define their One Core Market as Performance-Oriented Buyers + Cars and SUVs + Global + Premium.

SiteOrganic, the Internet pioneer mentioned in Chapter Three, defines their One Core Market as Churches and Ministries + websites + North America + Premium Value.

Your local coffee hangout might define their One Core Market as Social Neighbors + Coffee, Pastries and a Cool Hangout + the 20191 Zip Code + Value.

The recipe for disaster is a market defined as Everyone + Everything + Everywhere + Every Price Point.

Of course, there is one more question, which is, "Why?" The answer to the Why is your defining differentiation.

Decide One Thing. Align Everything. Win!

- Can you answer the four questions precisely?

- Is your definition uniquely yours?

- If not, consider shrinking your world.

PRICE POINTS

In every market, there are a broad range of answers to the "how much?" question.

The challenge for most organizations is to pick one.

We use a ten-part model to describe and delineate price points. You won't be surprised to learn that we use cars as the illustration.

1. Free: Hand-me-down junker

2. El Cheapo: Kia, Daewoo, Chery

3. Basic, No Frills: Subaru, Scion, Mazda

4. Value: Honda, Toyota, Chevrolet, VW, Ford

5. Premium Value: Acura, Lexus, Buick, Audi, Lincoln

6. Premium: BMW, Mercedes Benz, Cadillac

7. Ultra-Premium: Porsche, Lotus

8. Exclusive: Ferrari, Lamborghini

9. Ultra-Exclusive: Bentley, Maybach, Aston Martin

10. IYHTAYCAI*: Bugatti Veyron Super Sport

*If You Have To Ask, You Can't Afford It!

These descriptions and delineations are not perfect, but you can use them as a starting point to answer your "how much?" question. Our goal is for you to tailor them to your market.

Generally, companies and brands operate in one or maybe two of these price points.

For example, Toyotas are generally in the Value category. However, when Toyota moved upmarket, they created the new Lexus brand to do so. (People don't want to pay $60,000 for a Toyota—but gladly do so for a Lexus.)

And just in case you really want to know, the Bugatti Veyron Super Sport car is in the $2,400,000 range.

Decide One Thing. Align Everything. Win!

- How would you delineate the price points in your market?

- Which price point do you compete in?

- The middle price points are always the most crowded. Should you move up or down?

MAKE YOUR WORLD SMALLER

In *Good to Great* (2001), Jim Collins challenged leaders to identify something that they could become the "best in the world at."

Many organizations took Collins's advice, "confronted the brutal facts," and came to the demoralizing conclusion that they could not be the best in the world at anything.

After all, the world is a pretty big place.

And by definition, only one company can be the best.

To overcome this issue, we recommend a different approach.

While some organizations are chasing too many different markets, others have simply defined their market too broadly.

For example, we worked with one $10 million company which defined their target as a $3 billion market. Thus, they had a whopping 0.33 percent market share.

We advised them to narrow the market and find a niche that they could thoroughly understand and potentially dominate. As a rule of thumb, if your market share is not measured in the double digits, you have defined your market too broadly.

In addition, it is extremely difficult to break through and differentiate if you are a tiny player in a huge market.

By narrowing the focus, you make the world smaller.

This unlocks the possibility of becoming the best in your world.

For example, you may never be the best dry cleaner in the world—but perhaps you could become the best dry cleaner in the 20191 zip code.

You don't have a chance in a $3 billion market, but you could dominate a $300 million one.

Decide One Thing. Align Everything. Win!

- Have you defined your One Core Market too broadly?

- Is your market share measured in the double digits?

- If not, consider shrinking your world.

DON'T DABBLE...DOMINATE

You will never be differentiatingly great at One Thing if you are "all things to all people."

Thus, an organization must narrow its focus. This is a lot more difficult than it sounds, because many organizations are afraid that narrowing their focus will reduce revenue and growth.

In fact, just the opposite is true.

Selecting One Core Market allows organizations to develop exceptional, best-in-class insights about customers and their needs. This deep insight means that an organization is able to anticipate future needs better than their competitors.

Which drives innovation, further accelerating growth.

But you don't want to just select a market; you want to select the right market. There are hundreds of possibilities, but which is the best one?

To make the best decision, consider these critical questions:

- Is this a market segment that you do (or could) know cold—way better than anyone else?

- Is this a market segment that is growing?

- Is this market segment growing fast enough to support your revenue growth ambitions?

- Is this market segment big enough—but not too big?

- Is this market segment entrenched with established competitors?

- Can you dominate this market segment?

- Can you find a way to differentiate yourself?

Once you have answered these questions, you should be able to say, "We are intensely focused on the _____ market."

Decide One Thing. Align Everything. Win!

- Can you complete the "intensely focused" sentence?

- Why is that the best market for your organization?

- What adjacent markets will you be positioned to enter?

#ONE OR #TWO

Jack Welch, the former CEO of General Electric, was famous for his view that GE should be number one or number two in every market they competed in.

Otherwise, they should exit the market altogether.

While this advice has been circulating in the business world for decades, it seems timely to discuss it again.

At the heart of this sentiment is the idea that even GE, which competed in hundreds of markets, still had to choose. And that there were markets that even GE, with their vast resources, could not be successful in.

In our experience, most organizations compete in too many markets. But it takes incredible discipline not to chase every opportunity.

Just because you can enter a market doesn't mean that you should.

Remember: it is better to dominate One Market than dabble in a dozen of them.

But you also have to look beyond the top line. Just because a market generates revenue doesn't mean that it generates profit.

In addition, it is very common for organizations to underestimate the cost of entering new markets.

Even the Bible advises leaders to "count the costs."

Most organizations would be well served to reexamine the profitability of each market they compete in. Surprisingly, most of the clients we work with have never done this profitability analysis.

Beware: this exercise will create lots of interesting discussion about cost allocation. Creative finance types will make all kinds of arguments about how to divide the pie. Even so, the results will be revealing.

Rank all of the markets you compete in. Prune the worst, and reinvest in growing the best.

Who knows? Maybe you'll become #One or #Two.

Decide One Thing. Align Everything. Win!

- Are you #One or #Two in every market you compete in?

- If not, what will it take?

- Are there any markets that you should exit?

CHANGE THE RULES

Perhaps you have come to the realization that your organization can never become number one or number two in your market.

Then maybe it is time to change the rules.

Many of the organizations we profiled in Chapter Three created a new market or product category...and then went on to dominate the market they invented.

For example, Chipotle invented the "fast casual" category, and Red Bull invented the "extreme energy drink" category.

Some of the common strategies include:

- Invent an entirely new market.

- Create a new product category.

- Find a unique, undiscovered niche between two bigger segments.

- Merge two previously disconnected niches.

- Target an emerging but underserved demographic.

- Create an ultra-premium market in a stale category.

- Create an ultra-discount market by reinventing the cost model.

One of the best things about this process is you can define your market any way you want to.

After all, it is your market!

So don't be constrained by traditional market definitions and delineations. Be creative. Color outside the lines. Create your own game and make up all the rules.

Decide One Thing. Align Everything. Win!

- Is your thinking constrained by traditional market definitions and delineations?

- Are you trying to win a game that someone else invented?

- Which of the options seem best to you?

CHAPTER SIX

THE DECISION DRIVERS

BUYING DECISIONS ARE DRIVEN
BY MANY THINGS.

KNOWING YOUR CUSTOMERS

The most important thing an organization can do is to know their customers. Cold.

Unfortunately, most know far too little.

They assume and presume—often incorrectly.

In the last chapter, you defined your One Core Market, which is your unique combination of Who + What + Where + How Much.

Based on that definition, we must now go deep to understand what drives the customers' buying decisions.

Buying decisions are driven by many things and often are influenced by multiple stakeholders.

For business-to-business markets, start with understanding your customers' corporate issues, such as:

- Their vision, goals, and strategies

- Their CEO's top priorities

- Their competitive pressures

- Their economic engine

For all markets, also make sure you understand all of the stakeholders in the Decision-Making Unit, such as:

- The ultimate decision maker

- Key purchase influencers

Deciding which One Thing will be your defining differ-entiation requires a deep, comprehensive understand-ing of your customers' decision criteria, values, buying motives, decision-making process, and more.

Specifically, the process should seek to understand two groups of customers: current customers and wish-list customers.

Decide One Thing. Align Everything. Win!

- Do you really understand your customers' buying motives and decision drivers?

- Have you organized them into clusters?

- Is there one stakeholder in the Decision-Making Unit that is your primary target?

DECISION DRIVERS

....

When deciding to do business with your organization, customers consider many things.

These are decision drivers.

Some of the most common decision drivers include:

- Price

- Service

- Quality

- Reliability

- Features

- Terms and Conditions

- Customization

- Color

- Safety

- Size

- Convenience

- Experience

Make a comprehensive list of everything that your customers consider when evaluating your product or service. (Some lists will have thirty items or more!)

Many organizations have multiple products and services. Since our objective is to identify your corporate differentiation, it can be helpful to create this list for each product and service, and then consolidate the lists.

Decide One Thing. Align Everything. Win!

- Do you have a comprehensive list of decision drivers?

- Which ones are most important?

- Is there one that you are already known for?

CHAPTER SEVEN

DECISION TIME

THE ONE THING *EVERY* EXECUTIVE
TEAM MUST DECIDE IS...

WHAT IS YOUR ONE THING?

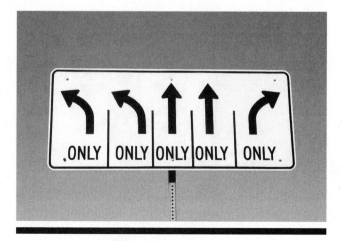

FIRST, BE GOOD AT EVERYTHING

The Decide One Thing process is about finding one of your customers' decision drivers that you can become differentiatingly great at.

But first, let's get real about just being good.

Satisfying today's demanding customers means that you have to be good at a lot of things. In fact, your solution must meet the minimum standards for all of the customers' decision drivers.

For example, if the customer values quality, then your quality must be good enough to meet their minimum quality standard.

If the customer values reliability, then your reliability must be good enough to meet their minimum reliability standard.

If the customer values service, then you must answer the phone!

When confronted with the list of decision drivers, many organizations conclude that they fall short in several areas. These organizations have some significant improvements to make just to be good.

Of course, determining exactly what the minimally acceptable level of performance is can be complicated.

In some areas, there is a clear industry benchmark or measurable target.

For example, when it comes to car safety, the government's crash testing gives a clear industry benchmark for every vehicle. While safety might not be number one on a car buyer's shopping list, everyone expects their cars to meet the minimum.

For other areas, the definition of the minimally acceptable level of performance might be fuzzy and subjective.

For example, just how clean do a restaurant's bathrooms need to be? Obviously, this can be very subjective. One person's good enough is another person's disgusting.

Decide One Thing. Align Everything. Win!

- Rate your organization's performance—from poor to world-class for each of the decision drivers.

- Does your organization meet "minimum standards" for each decision driver?

- If not, how can you upgrade your performance ASAP?

NEXT, DECIDE ONE THING

Once you have confirmed that you are at least good at everything the customer values, it is time to decide which One of them you can become differentiatingly great at.

Decisions, decisions.

For some organizations, the decision will be obvious right away. Sometimes, it has been part of the vision and DNA from the very beginning.

For most organizations, however, this process will be much more iterative.

Taking a long hard look in the mirror can help. For example:

- Look at your driving passion. Often, this comes directly from the organization's founder. Steve Jobs was obsessive about simplifying the man-machine interface from the very beginning of Apple.

- Look at your strengths. Start with a list of what you do best and then see if there is one that you can become differentiatingly great at. Dyson turned a strength in innovation into a global empire.

- Look at your assets. These can be physical assets, such as manufacturing plants, or intangible assets, such as intellectual property.

At Signature, their manufacturing plant was the surprise answer.

- Look at your values. The founders of BTI360 had "developing people" as one of their core values. Now, it has become the firm's defining differentiation.

- Look at your distinctives. Heritage is the only conservative think tank with the breadth required to lay out an integrated, ten-point Leadership for America agenda.

- Look at your economic engine. At Bognet Construction, an analysis of project profitability confirmed that their most profitable projects were the ones where they were the most proactive.

- Look at your wins and losses. At SiteOrganic, the win/loss analysis was the key insight that led to defining their ideal customer as "ministry innovators for whom the Internet is strategically important."

Evaluating the options and coming to a final decision is ultimately the responsibility of the executive team.

Decide One Thing. Align Everything. Win!

- What are your top three One Thing candidates?
- What are the pros and cons of each one?
- How will you decide?

CHECK POINTS

Deciding which One Thing will be the organization's defining differentiation is the most important decision that an executive team has to make.

However, leaders often worry that they will pick the wrong thing.

In virtually every case, the Decide One Thing process is iterative. Executive teams develop an initial hypothesis and "try it on for size." Then, there are periods of refinement. Ultimately, a winning idea emerges.

Consider the following ten Check Points to validate whether your One Thing is the right one for your organization.

1. Illuminating: It provides long-term strategic direction.

2. Compelling: The customer values it (and is willing to pay for it!).

3. Winning: The competitors can't match it.

4. Energizing: It puts "high octane" fuel in everyone's tank.

5. Defining: It defines who you are (and who you want to be).

6. Focusing: It focuses energy on what you can become great at.

7. Unifying: It brings the entire organization together.

8. Capitalizing: It leverages your unique strengths and assets.

9. Driving: It drives the bottom line.

10. Prioritizing: It guides where to invest and where to harvest.

If you score a perfect 10, then you are on your way to greatness.

If not, perhaps your hypothesis needs some more disciplined thought.

Decide One Thing. Align Everything. Win!

• Did your One Thing pass the test?

• If so, are there any areas that still need refining?

• If not, keep working on it!

THE DECISION

Based on our analysis and input from key stakeholders, we have decided to become differentiatingly great at

_____.

This is our One Thing.

CHAPTER EIGHT

ALIGN EVERYTHING

DECIDING ONE THING IS ONE THING.

ALIGNING YOUR ORGANIZATION TO
ACTUALLY DELIVER IT IS ANOTHER THING.

THE DISCIPLINE OF ALIGNMENT

Whether your company has 2 people or 200,000, aligning them into one differentiation-driven organization is essential to success.

Imagine an organization in which:

- Every employee sees the vision. No myopia.

- Every employee has bought in to the strategy. No naysayers.

- Everyone puts "we before me." No underminers.

- Every employee is committed to the mission. No laggards.

- Every employee lives the organization's values. No backstabbers.

- Every process is optimized. No time-wasters.

- Every customer is engaged. No complainers.

To achieve these results, you must apply the discipline of alignment.

As the name implies, aligning thousands of different people and dozens of disparate systems takes discipline.

And real clarity about exactly what you want to align around.

Your One Thing can provide exactly the clarity that organizations need to bring everything—and everyone—into alignment. (SHIFTPOINTS uses a "100 Points of Alignment" model.)

As MJ Wivell from BTI360 says, "Once you have your One Thing, it is really easy to tell whether something is aligned or not."

Building a fully aligned organization is not impossible, but they are extremely rare. Normally, you'll find them in the winner's circle.

Decide One Thing. Align Everything. Win!

- How aligned is your organization?

- Do you agree that a fully aligned organization is really possible?

- How can the executive team provide the discipline that is required?

THE CHIEF ALIGNMENT OFFICER

Organizations don't just naturally align themselves. It takes an intentional focus on the issue. Someone has to make it happen.

We call this person your "Chief Alignment Officer."

Some of the tasks of the Chief Alignment Officer include:

- Ensuring that everything and everyone is aligned with your One Thing.

- Ensuring that the vision is clear and articulated in an inspiring way.

- Ensuring that values are clearly codified and enforced.

- Ensuring that the goals and targets are clearly defined and cascaded to every person.

- Ensuring that the strategic annual and quarterly plans are focused and aligned.

- Ensuring that the organization is structured to deliver the strategy.

- Ensuring that the organization is hiring the right people and deploying them wisely.

- Ensuring that the right behaviors and results are being recognized and rewarded.

- Ensuring that the marketing messages are clear, compelling, and in alignment with the strategy.

- Ensuring that the customer is boss, and that the organization is focused on what really matters to the customer.

- Ensuring that the measurement systems measure what really matters.

This is a big job, but your transformation into a differentiation-driven organization depends on it.

Choose wisely.

Decide One Thing. Align Everything. Win!

- Does your organization have someone functioning as the Chief Alignment Officer?

- Has that person been empowered to confront fragmentation?

- Is it working?

THE A-TEAM

Having a Chief Alignment Officer is important, but that person can't do it alone.

You also must call in the A-Team.

The Alignment Team (A-Team) is comprised of leaders empowered to bring the organization into alignment. They must have the organizational credibility and political capital to build coalitions and break down barriers.

The Chief Alignment Officer and the A-Team will create an "Alignment Factory," which will systematically and rigorously drive the process.

The "Wall of Shame" will highlight the messaging inconsistencies and provide a visible representation of the campaign. It is a great way to show the "before" and "after."

Aligning documents, systems, or processes is relatively easy. But aligning people is hard. Therefore, it is critical to pay special attention to people issues.

Every employee will have questions about what the One Thing means to him or her.

To buy in to the idea, employees must know why you are making the change, what is in it for them, and exactly what you expect them to do now.

Answering these legitimate questions will help people "climb the buy-in ladder."

The A-Team will also build and maintain momentum with a steady stream of wins and validations. Delivering early wins is a must. Celebrating them publicly will generate momentum, but avoid declaring victory too early.

Many programs start out well, but hit a wall. Easy issues are resolved first; difficult ones are procrastinated.

Success requires endurance and a long-term perspective.

According to virtually every study ever conducted on organizational change, 70% of change initiatives fail to achieve their objectives.

Calling in the A-Team will dramatically improve your chance of success.

Decide One Thing. Align Everything. Win!

- Is your organization highly aligned or highly fragmented?

- How has growth impacted your alignment?

- Are things getting better or worse?

ONE #ONE PRIORITY

The word "priority" came into the English language in the fourteenth century. However, it wasn't until the twentieth century that it was pluralized.

Perhaps it is redundant to say, "One #One Priority," but some organizations have so many priorities that everything is a priority. Too often, organizations even have competing, contradictory priorities.

So, if you can only have One Priority, what should it be?

Your One Priority should be to become truly, differentiatingly great at your One Thing.

Of course, this means that every other thing is a lesser priority.

To become truly, differentiatingly great, organizations must:

- Invest in programs essential to your One Thing, and rationalize those that aren't.

- Target markets that value your One Thing, and exit markets that don't.

- Develop products that showcase your One Thing, and prune products that don't.

- Optimize the processes that deliver your One Thing, and marginalize those that don't.

- Recognize people who "get" your One Thing, and have conversations with those who don't.

Each of these actions—and countless others—are required of those on the road to greatness.

And achieving true greatness takes a really long time—perhaps a decade or more. Some will start the journey and quit. Others will hit turbulence and lose their nerve.

But a few will make One Thing their #One Priority for One Decade … or as long as it takes.

Decide One Thing. Align Everything. Win!

- What is your organization's #One Priority now?

- How can you leverage your One Thing to drive change?

- Which markets, products, or people need to be pruned?

THE ONE NUMBER

....

Organizations track and evaluate many metrics in order to get a complete view of performance, but high-performers identify One Number as the way to keep score.

Because you can't win if your team doesn't know the score.

The problem with most dashboards is that they are too complex. They present a mind-numbing array of information—most of it useful, but too often it distracts focus away from the most important information.

Consider baseball.

A player's batting average is useful information. His batting average against left-handed pitchers is useful. His batting average against left-handed pitchers in night games is useful. His batting average against left-handed pitchers in night games with runners in scoring position is useful. I guess that his batting average against left-handed pitchers in night games with runners in scoring position during the month of October might be useful as well.

But the only number that really matters in baseball is the final score.

Smart leaders know that simplifying the metrics down to One Number makes it possible for every employee to know exactly what the goals are, how those goals are measured, and how every employee's job fits in.

Lots of numbers are important, but it is the job of the leader to define which one is the most important.

Therefore, one of a leader's greatest challenges is to define the right measure of success.

Revenue. Revenue growth. Profitability. Market share. Customer satisfaction. Net Promoter. Employee engagement. Human Sigma. Economic value added. Return on assets. Utilization rate. Earnings per share. Net worth. All of these (and more) are good numbers.

Which one is the most important for your organization?

That depends on your One Thing.

Decide One Thing. Align Everything. Win!

- What is your One Number?

- What is your current performance level?

- What is the target performance level?

TRACTION MANAGEMENT

My BMW has a very sophisticated all-wheel drive traction management system. In any road condition, the car is simply unstoppable.

Traction is what converts RPM into MPH!

In many organizations, change initiatives simply are not getting traction. They have the pedal to the metal, but they just aren't getting anywhere.

Lots of RPM—but not much MPH.

Like a car's traction management system, your One Thing will enable you to:

- Transfer organizational power and resources to the initiatives that have the greatest promise.

- Prune activities that are distractions or delusions.

- Double-down on the markets that you have a reasonable chance of dominating.

- Exit the markets that you are simply dabbling in.

- Terminate the bottom performers, so you can reinvest time and energy in your very best people.

- Accelerate decision-making.

- Optimize the mission-critical organizational processes.

Turbulent times and uncertain economic outlooks are the equivalent of icy winter storms. To get to your destination, you'll need a sophisticated traction management system.

This is precisely what your One Thing will provide.

Without it, you'll just keep spinning your wheels.

Decide One Thing. Align Everything. Win!

- Do your strategic initiatives have the traction required to succeed?

- What has been the impact of economic turbulence?

- Is your organization just "spinning its wheels"?

MIXED SIGNALS

In the 1997 Indy 500, Tony Stewart hit the wall on lap 198 (of 200). His accident brought out the yellow flag.

On lap 199, the starter waved the green flag, indicating that the race was back on, but the track lights still showed yellow, indicating that the race was still in a caution.

Arie Luyendyk saw the green flag and hit the gas, but Scott Goodyear saw the yellow lights and hesitated, which essentially killed his chance of winning.

Mixed signals cost Scott Goodyear the Indy 500.

Unfortunately, organizations send these kinds of mixed signals all the time.

- The posters proclaim your core values, but the interview guide has a different list.

- The marketing campaign promises an integrated solution, but the proposal boilerplate doesn't.

- The mission statement extols teamwork, but the compensation plan only rewards individual performance.

And just like mixed signals caused Scott Goodyear to lose the Indy 500, they cause organizations to dramatically underperform their potential.

However, now that you have Decided One Thing, you can use it as a catalyst for aligning all of your messages. We call this—not surprisingly—your One Message.

Here is how the process works.

Write about three dozen great sentences that describe your One Thing and bring the idea to life.

Take an inventory of all of your documents and communications vehicles—job descriptions, sales proposals, Web content … everything.

Prioritize the list and simply start updating everything, infusing the One Thing message while eliminating ideas that contradict or confuse.

Pretty soon, all of your lights will be green.

Decide One Thing. Align Everything. Win!

- Are some of your lights green, while others are flashing yellow?

- Are some of your people hesitating to commit, waiting for you to clarify the message?

- Are you willing to confront the issues?

CHAPTER NINE

WINNING THE RACE

IF YOUR ONE THING IS JUST A TAGLINE, IT WON'T DO ANYTHING. BUT IF IT IS A CATALYST FOR INSTITUTIONALIZED GREATNESS, IT DOES EVERYTHING.

WINNING
THE RACE

DIFFERENTIATINGLY GREAT

I spent twenty-five years in the technology business. So I could not help but notice that Verizon is running ads with the following tagline:

"The business with the best technology rules."

Catchy. But is it true?

Is an organization's technology really the thing that gives them a differentiating competitive advantage? Or is it their products? Or their service? Or their cost infrastructure? Or their brand? Or their supply chain?

By now, you know the answer.

The organization that finds their One Thing and then becomes differentiatingly great at delivering it is the one that rules.

Of course, for some organizations, technology will be the One Thing.

If technology is indeed your One Thing, invest as much as you can to transform your technology infrastructure into a differentiating competitive advantage. Technology leadership should drive everything. Technology investments should get the highest priority. You should only hire geeks.

However, for most organizations, the One Thing will be something else. And you will need to align everything—and everyone—in your organization with your One Thing.

If customer service is your One Thing, you must answer the phone on the first ring. Your front line people must be empowered to solve problems. You should make heroes of those who go the extra mile. Hire humble people with servants' hearts.

If design is your One Thing, invest in office space that inspires creativity. Buy cool furniture. Support the arts. Hire the most unique mix of people you can and get out of their way.

If price is your One Thing, focus on lowering your cost structure. Recycle paperclips. Hire tightwads.

Sorry, Verizon. Organizations that Decide One Thing and then align everything are the ones who rule.

Decide One Thing. Align Everything. Win!

- Is technology your organization's One Thing?

- If so, have you invested enough to become differentiatingly great?

- If technology is not your One Thing, should your IT investments be pruned?

WHERE THE RUBBER
MEETS THE ROAD

Promising One Thing is one thing. Delivering it Every Time is another thing!

This is where the rubber meets the road.

Every year, organizations spend billions on marketing, making promises to customers. To cut through the clutter and stand out from the competition, their claims get bigger and more audacious. Every day, salespeople make promises to customers. To win the deal, their promises get bolder and more exaggerated.

And customers make purchase decisions based on these heightened promises. Too often, what customers actually experience is a far cry from what the organization promised. We call this the "Customer Experience Gap."

In contrast, differentiation-driven organizations apply fanatical attention to detail, building a firm that "promises exactly what they deliver, and delivers exactly what they promise."

Not one time, but Every Time.

All of the research confirms the correlation between employee engagement and customer satisfaction.

To deliver every time, these two processes must be managed in an integrated fashion.

The process starts with recruiting, developing, and unleashing the talents of exceptional people.

Great managers must keep the engagement, motivation, and enthusiasm level sky-high.

A great television commercial for Samuel Adams beer captures this idea perfectly.

"Happy employees make better beer!"

In addition, you must optimize your value-delivery processes. Start by identifying every "moment of truth" in their transaction lifecycle. A moment of truth occurs anytime you interact with a customer. In most organizations, there are hundreds of these moments of truth during the course of a transaction.

Decide One Thing. Align Everything. Win!

- Do happy employees really make better beer?

- Who comes first, employees or customers?

- Which processes are mission critical to delivering your One Thing?

COPYCATS

When I was a kid, our cat scratched me in the eye. So I don't like cats.

But I hate copycats.

Once you Decide One Thing, competitors can—and probably will—copy your words.

- "Our vacuums don't lose suction either!"
- "Our tomatoes are fresh too."
- "Our cars have great performance too."

However, your One Thing is not about words, which can easily be copied.

It is about institutionalizing the millions of things that are required for you to become differentiatingly great.

Of course, you should also invest in protecting the unique intellectual property associated with your One Thing. After all, there is a reason that the recipe for the secret sauce is a secret.

BMW has invested millions of hours perfecting their unique driving experience. Apple has invested millions of hours perfecting their unique user experience. Walmart has invested millions of hours perfecting their unique supply chain. Lexus has invested millions of hours perfecting perfection.

Others have tried to copy them, but always fall short.

Their greatness is institutionalized into every molecule of their organizations.

Every process is optimized to deliver One Thing. Every person is passionate about One Thing. Every product is infused with One Thing. Every message is aligned to say One Thing. Every investment is rationalized to advance One Thing.

If your One Thing is just a tagline, it won't do anything. But if it is a catalyst for institutionalized greatness, it does everything.

Decide One Thing. Align Everything. Win!

- Which competitor is most likely to copy your One Thing?

- How will you respond?

- How can you protect your intellectual property?

0.043 OF A SECOND

Hanging in my garage is one of my prized possessions. It is a lithograph of the closest finish in the history of the Indianapolis 500, given to me by my friend, race car driver and television commentator Scott Goodyear.

In the 1992 Indy 500, Scott Goodyear started the race in thirty-third position.

Otherwise known as last.

For two and a half hours, Scott put in the laps. He let the crazy, impatient drivers crash or burn out their cars. Slowly but surely, he climbed up the leaderboard.

Five hundred miles later, Scott crossed the finish line just 0.043 of a second behind the winner, Al Unser Jr. Scott didn't win, but the race is a great testimony to his persistence and tenacity.

Persistence and tenacity. Characteristics of winning race car drivers … and differentiation-driven organizations.

Jim Collins confirms this idea in *Good to Great*, in which he talks about the long build-up phase that precedes the breakthrough. In fact, our client experience has confirmed this phenomenon.

Building a differentiation-driven organization is a long-term project. There will be many times when the efforts don't seem to be paying off.

Investments with no return. Pain without gain.

But if you are on the journey to building a differentiation-driven organization, be persistent.

Make progress every day. Be tenacious. Overcome obstacles (and competitors). Don't let the naysayers get you off track.

Decide One Thing. Align Everything. Win!

- What are your critical areas of performance improvement?

- How long will it take to achieve your goal?

- Are you willing to stay in the race for the long term?

ACCELERATING CLARITY

In today's turbulent times, there is a tremendous amount of anxiety. Leaders are faced with unprecedented competition. Business models are made obsolete overnight. Entire industries are being restructured by one deal. All of this anxiety can cause organizations to grind to a halt.

The antidote for anxiety is clarity.

When you decide which One Thing will be your defining differentiation, it provides "accelerating clarity."

- It provides accelerating clarity to your vision.

- It provides accelerating clarity to your strategy.

- It provides accelerating clarity for your people.

- It provides accelerating clarity about who to hire and who to fire.

- It provides accelerating clarity about where to invest and where to prune.

- It provides accelerating clarity about how (and what) to manage.

- It provides accelerating clarity about what products and services to build.

- It provides accelerating clarity about what markets to enter (and exit).

- It provides accelerating clarity for customers … since they know exactly what to expect.

All this from just One Thing? Yes!

And trust us; providing accelerating clarity is way better than experiencing "decelerating ambiguity."

Decide One Thing. Align Everything. Win!

- How clear is your messaging?

- Does everything work together to deliver One Message?

- Does your organization operate with results-accelerating clarity?

CHAPTER TEN

THE WINNER'S CIRCLE

TIME TO KISS SOME BRICKS!

KISSING BRICKS

I sat on the start/finish line in row eight for the 2012 Indy 500, and had a front-row seat to one of the most unusual traditions in sports.

Kissing bricks.

After winning the race, Dario Franchitti came out to the middle of the track, knelt down, and kissed the famous one-yard-wide strip of bricks that marks the start/finish line.

Traditions like these make the Indianapolis Motor Speedway special.

Great organizations use traditions—like kissing bricks—to build a high-performance culture.

We started this book talking about organizations that were at a shift point.

If your executive team has completed the Decide One Thing...Align Everything...Win process, congratulations.

You deserve credit for accomplishing something great.

Time to kiss some bricks.

BUT WAIT...
THERE'S
MORE!

THE ULTIMATE SHIFT POINT

In the 1997 Indy 500, Arie Luyendyk was the fastest qualifier, at 218.263 miles per hour, which earned him the coveted pole position. Arie was fast all day, led 61 of the 200 laps, and went on to win the race, just 0.7 seconds ahead of his teammate Scott Goodyear.

It was an exciting day for Team Nortel, with our cars finishing first and second. When Arie drank the milk, I was standing just a few feet away. It was an unbelievable experience celebrating with the entire team.

Winning the race is great...but it is critical to choose the right race.

There are lots of races to choose from.

Some are focused on the race to the top, and define winning by their title.

Some are focused on the race for wealth, and define winning by their net worth.

Others are focused on the race for fame, and define winning by how many Twitter followers they have.

After many years running these races, I came to the Ultimate Shift Point. I was redlined, and knew that I was running the wrong race.

I was in the fast lane on the road to nowhere.

God intervened and illuminated my path. He showed me the way. He introduced me to His Son.

This led to a complete transformation of my goals, priorities, and worldview. I redefined success and now live with an eternal perspective. I'm on a different road, running a different race for different reasons. At the end of my race, I look forward to that "fifth left turn" into Jesus' presence.

For me, it was the Ultimate Shift Point.

Decide One Thing. Align Everything. Win!

- Are you running the right race?

- Are you living with an eternal perspective?

- At the checkered flag, are you going to make the fifth left turn?

SHIFTPOINTS TOOLBOX

We've all joked about the crazy late-night infomercials that try to sweeten the deal with the famous line,

"But wait, there's more!"

In the spirit of over-delivering, we have many other tools to help accelerate your transformation into a differentiation-driven organization.

You'll find them on the SHIFTPOINTS website. Just click on the Red Toolbox, and you will find:

- Speed Readings: One-page summaries of key SHIFTPOINTS concepts.

- SHIFTPOINTS: Our blog about building differentiation-driven organizations. We post new entries every Monday morning. You can read them online, or subscribe at SHIFTPOINTS.com/blog. As in this book, we cover a wide range of topics, from differentiation to winning.

- Check Points: Surveys to help you assess your organization. They cover everything from differentiation to alignment to the performance of your executive team. Most of them feature "ten easy questions."

- The SHIFTPOINTS Differentiation Index assessment: To start the process, contact us at start@SHIFTPOINTS.com.

- Winner's Circle: Case studies about organizations that have implemented the Decide One Thing... Align Everything...Win model.

Decide One Thing. Align Everything. Win!

- You can learn more about SHIFTPOINTS at www.SHIFTPOINTS.com.

- You can subscribe to the blog at www.SHIFTPOINTS.com/blog.

- You can learn more about me at www.daveramos.com.

THANK YOU

....

Of course, many people helped and encouraged me along the way. I have much to be thankful for, and many people to thank.

Thanks to my Lord. I pray that He is glorified by my work.

Thanks to Ken Thornton, for challenging me to write a book.

Thanks to my mom, who always told me, "*David kann alles.*" You never stopped believing that.

Thanks to my wife Twee, who was a sounding board for hundreds of ideas.

Thanks to Jennifer Whittenberg, who has been with me since the beginning. You are the best. I'll never forget how much you have done for me.

Thanks to Barbara Israel, who has proofread everything I've ever written. Poor Barbara!

Thanks to my friend and *New York Times* bestselling author Joel Rosenberg. You thanked me in your first book. Back at you. Get the boys praying for a bestseller!

Thanks to our clients, who taught me so much. You were a living lab for our ideas. I'd especially like to thank:

- Jim and Jennifer Bognet, from Bognet Construction—you've been with me the longest and taught me about being Relentlessly Proactive.

- Brad Hill, from SiteOrganic—you were the first to Decide One Thing and inspired me to Produce Fruit.

- MJ Wivell and Jeremy Nimtz, from BTI360—your commitment to Developing Ultimate Teammates is an exemplar that every organization should follow.

- Jim Brady and the Group W geniuses—you made me bring my A-game and pushed and prodded until we came up with The Right Answer.

- Michael Tinsley, Rob Wilson, and the NeoSystems team—Grow Ahead … you are on your way to realizing the 2020 Vision.

Thanks to the SHIFTPOINTS Advisory Board, which held me accountable and championed our cause.

Thanks to our many friends, partners, and like-minded consultants who were a sounding board for all of these ideas.

Godspeed.

ABOUT THE AUTHOR

Dave Ramos is the founder and CEO of SHIFTPOINTS, Inc.

Prior to founding SHIFTPOINTS, Dave built differentiation-driven organizations in a broad range of settings, including large global corporations, venture-backed start-ups, and innovative nonprofits.

He held executive positions with global leaders like Nortel Networks, where he was the Vice President of Global Marketing. At Nortel, Dave won the company's highest award, The Chairman's Award, for innovations in marketing. At IBM, Dave won the company's highest award, The Golden Circle, for innovations in sales.

He was employee #13 at AnswerLogic, a venture-backed software company, where he led sales, marketing, and business development.

After AnswerLogic, Dave spent four years doing pro bono consulting, volunteer work, and teaching.

One of his consulting clients, McLean Bible Church (a 15,000 person megachurch) asked him to join the staff full time. Surprising everyone, Dave accepted the job. He spent three years as the Director of Adult Ministries and led the church through a strategic alignment initiative.

He left the MBC staff to start The Dashboard Group, which changed its name to SHIFTPOINTS in January, 2013.

Dave has an MBA from the Harvard Business School, and a BS in accounting from Drexel University. He serves on the Board of Directors for Fellowship of Christian Athletes Golf Ministry and Workforce Ministries.

Dave is a sought-after speaker, and engages audiences with his humorous yet challenging style. He has spoken at organizations such as The Harvard Business School, Nyack College, Vistage, Convene Now, The CXO Forum, AOL, and many churches and ministries around the country.

Dave is good at a lot of things, but is working to become differentiatingly great at his One Thing.

How can you use this book?

MOTIVATE

EDUCATE

THANK

INSPIRE

PROMOTE

CONNECT

Why have a custom version of *Decide One Thing*?

- Build personal bonds with customers, prospects, employees, donors, and key constituencies

- Develop a long-lasting reminder of your event, milestone, or celebration

- Provide a keepsake that inspires change in behavior and change in lives

- Deliver the ultimate "thank you" gift that remains on coffee tables and bookshelves

- Generate the "wow" factor

Books are thoughtful gifts that provide a genuine sentiment that other promotional items cannot express. They promote employee discussions and interaction, reinforce an event's meaning or location, and they make a lasting impression. Use your book to say "Thank You" and show people that you care.

Decide One Thing is available in bulk quantities and in customized versions at special discounts for corporate, institutional, and educational purposes. To learn more please contact our Special Sales team at:

1.866.775.1696 • sales@advantageww.com • wwwAdvantageSpecialSales.com